15

D033676S

IT'S AMAZING!
DINOSAURS

Annabel Savery

W
FRANKLIN WATTS
LONDON·SYDNEY

First published in 2011 by
Franklin Watts
338 Euston Road
London NW1 3BH

Franklin Watts Australia
Level 17/207 Kent Street
Sydney NSW 2000

A CIP catalogue record for this book is available from the British Library.

Planning and production by Discovery Books Limited
Managing editor: Laura Durman
Editor: Annabel Savery
Designer: Ian Winton

Picture credits: Dinosaurcentral.com, Mineo Shiraishi: p. 16, p. 20, p. 21 top, p. 21 bottom, p. 26 top; Getty Images: p. 6 (Dorling Kindersley), p. 10 (Ira Block), p. 13 bottom (KAZUHIRO NOGI/Staff/AFP), p. 15 top (Mario Tama/Staff), p. 18 right, p. 19 (Highlights for Children), p. 22 (De Agostini Picture Library/Contributor), p. 29 (Oli Scarff/Staff); iStockPhoto.com: p. 8 top (benedek), p. 27 top (SoopySue); Photoshot: p. 28 (Universal Pictures); Shutterstock Images: title & p. 17 bottom & p. 23 (Andreas Meyer), p. 4 & p. 5 top & p. 7 top & p. 12 (all Linda Bucklin), p. 5 bottom (Vaclav Volrab), p. 7 bottom (Neo Edmund), p. 8 bottom (Styve Reineck), p. 9 (alexal), p. 11 top (JCElv), p. 11 bottom (Catmando), p. 13 top (Jean-Michel Girard), p. 14 (Piotr Marcinski), p. 15 bottom (Vaclav Volrab), p. 17 top (BORTEL Pavel), p. 18 left (Krzysztof Wiktor), p. 24 (beboy), p. 25 (Triff), p. 26 bottom (Volodymyr Krasyuk), p. 27 bottom (Vital Che).

Cover photo: Shutterstock (Sakala)

A CIP catalogue record for this book is available from the British Library.

Dewey Decimal Classification Number: 567.9

ISBN 978 1 4451 0548 2

Franklin Watts is a division of Hachette Children's Books,
an Hachette UK company.
www.hachette.co.uk

Printed in China

CONTENTS

All words in **bold** appear in the glossary on page 30.

THE DINOSAURS

For millions of years, creatures known as dinosaurs roamed freely on Earth.

Dicraeosaurus
(length: up to 20 m)

Dinosaurs lived more than
220 million years ago.

IT'S AMAZING!

There were more than 1,000 different types of dinosaur. Not all of them were enormous. Some, such as the compsognathus, were the same size as chickens!

Compsognathus
(length: up to 65 cm)

For a long time, scientists thought that dinosaurs were a type of **reptile.**

However, reptiles are **cold-blooded** and scientists now think that dinosaurs were **warm-blooded.** This makes them more like **mammals.**

Stegosaurus
(length:
up to 9 m)

DINOSAUR TIMES

When the dinosaurs were alive 220 million years ago the Earth looked very different from the way it does now.

Millions of years ago the **continents** were all joined together into one supercontinent. Over time, the land broke up into separate pieces.

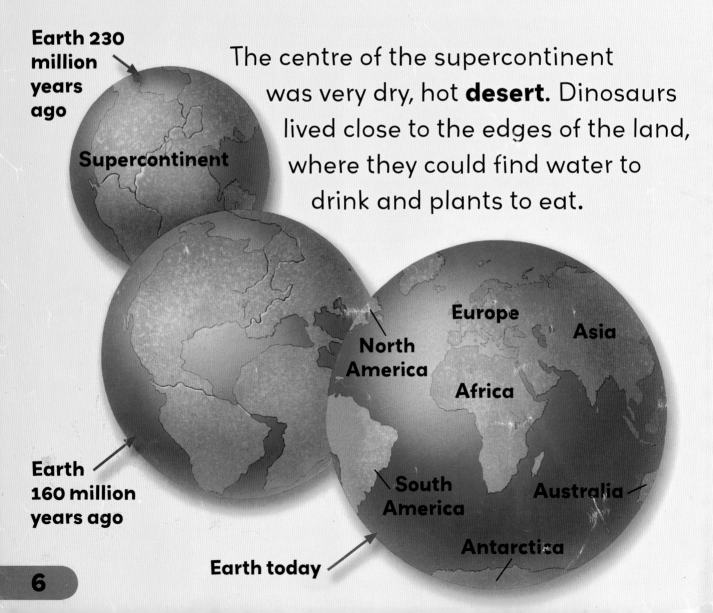

Earth 230 million years ago

Supercontinent

The centre of the supercontinent was very dry, hot **desert**. Dinosaurs lived close to the edges of the land, where they could find water to drink and plants to eat.

Europe

Asia

North America

Africa

Earth 160 million years ago

South America

Australia

Antarctica

Earth today

As the supercontinent broke apart, the sea divided the land. The **climate** became much warmer and wetter. This meant that plants could grow in more places and dinosaurs could live in more places, too.

Buzzing about!

When flowering plants started growing on the Earth, other creatures, such as bees and butterflies, appeared too.

FANTASTIC FOSSILS

So how do we know that dinosaurs once lived on Earth? It's because of fossils!

Fossils are the remains of animals or plants that have been buried in mud or soil for millions of years. Over time, the mud or soil turns to stone and protects the remains like a case. Fossils are studied by scientists called **palaeontologists.**

Fossils

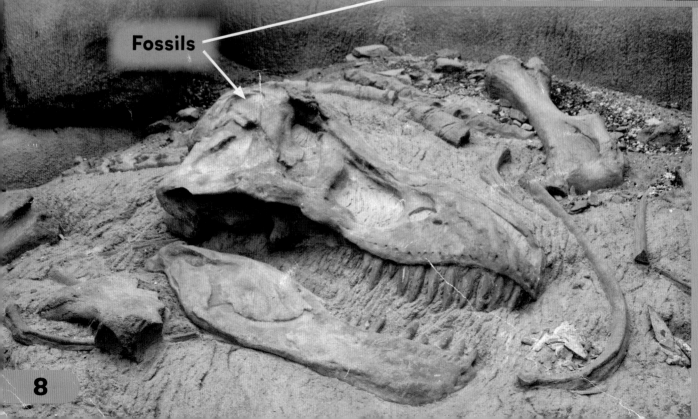

When palaeontologists collect enough fossilised bones from one type of dinosaur, they piece them together like a jigsaw puzzle. This makes a whole skeleton.

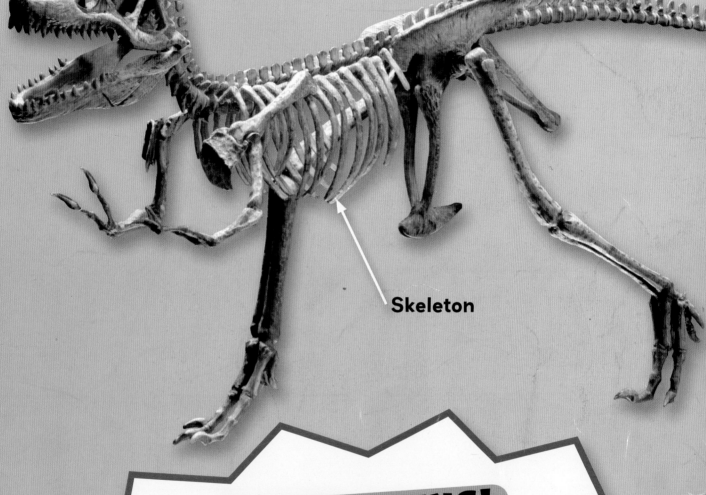

Skeleton

IT'S AMAZING!

One of the biggest finds was a neck bone of a dinosaur called a seismosaurus. It was over 1.8 m long. This means that the actual dinosaur would have been more than 40 m long. The bone was found in New Mexico, USA.

THE PLANT EATERS

Dinosaurs that ate plants are known as **herbivores**.

Grinding teeth

Most herbivores had lots of small, rough teeth. These teeth were good for grinding up plants.

Nigersaurus (length: up to 15 m)

Teeth

Each herbivore only ate certain types of food. The nigersaurus ate grass and small plants. It had very wide jaws with more than 600 small, sharp teeth.

The diplodocus and the brachiosaurus both had really long necks. This meant that they could reach up to eat the leaves on tall trees.

Brachiosaurus (length: up to 30 m)

IT'S AMAZING!

A diplodocus' neck could be as long as 8 m, and a brachiosaurus' neck could be even longer!

Diplodocus (length: up to 26 m)

THE MEAT EATERS

The main **predators** that dinosaurs had to watch out for were other dinosaurs! These were the meat-eaters, or **carnivores**.

Tyrannosaurus rex had a good sense of smell, so it was an excellent hunter. It could also run very fast, at up to 32 kilometres per hour, and could easily catch other dinosaurs like these compsognathus.

Tyrannosaurus rex (length: up to 12 m)

Compsognathus (length: up to 65 cm)

Allosaurus was another fierce hunter.

It was more than 10 m long and had very sharp teeth in its large jaws.

Allosaurus (length: up to 12 m)

The terrifying megaraptor (below), had long, sharp claws for slicing open its **prey.** Its longest claw would have been about 35 cm long!

Claws

Razor teeth

Meat-eating dinosaurs had teeth especially designed for biting through tough skin and muscle. The teeth were very sharp and serrated, like a bread-knife.

ARMOURED DINOSAURS

Many dinosaurs had hard, bone-like plates on their skin to protect them.

Triceratops (below) looked a bit like a modern rhinoceros. The word triceratops means 'three-horned face'.

The dinosaur had three horns on its head and a wide, bone **plate** to protect its neck.

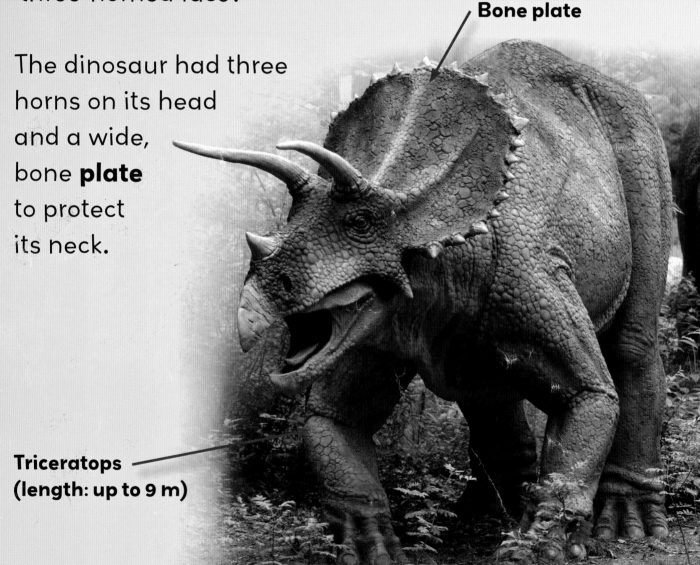

Bone plate

Triceratops
(length: up to 9 m)

Stygimoloch (right) had lots of horns on its head to make it look fierce. Stygimoloch was part of a group known as the bone-headed dinosaurs. These dinosaurs used their bony heads to strike their attackers in a fight.

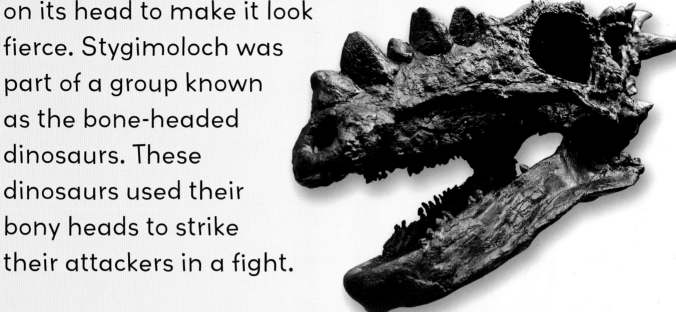

IT'S AMAZING!

The ankylosaurus probably had the most armour of all the dinosaurs. It had plates on its skin (even around its eyes), spikes on its back, horns on its head and a tail like a club!

Ankylosaurus
(length: up to 7 m)

STRANGE DINOSAURS

Dinosaurs were all shapes and sizes. Here are some strange examples.

The saurolophus had a long piece of bone sticking up on its head. This was attached to a flap of skin that could be blown up.

The flap might have been used to make noise, or just to show off to other dinosaurs!

Saurolophus (length: up to 9 m)

The stegosaurus had big bony plates along its back. These may have been used to protect the stegosaurus against predators. They may also have been used to cool the dinosaur down, or take in heat from the Sun.

Stegosaurus (length: up to 9 m)

The spinosaurus

The spinosaurus had a fin on its back made of spines with skin in between. It stood up when the dinosaur arched its back. The fin alone was the height of a tall human!

Spinosaurus (length: up to 18 m)

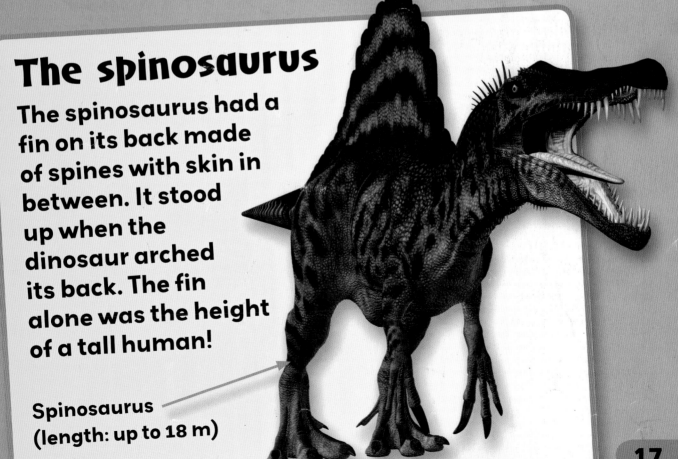

THE BIGGEST AND SMALLEST

There were big dinosaurs... and small dinosaurs.

One of the largest carnivores that has been found is the gigantosaurus. It was 12.5 m long!

Microraptor (length: up to 80 cm)

The microraptor was one of the smallest dinosaurs. It was not much bigger than a chicken, but had a very long tail. Its arms and legs were both covered with feathers.

Gigantosaurus (length: up to 12.5 m)

The titanosaurs were a group of huge dinosaurs. The largest was the argentinosaurus. It measured an incredible 35 m from nose to tail. That's about the length of seven medium-sized cars!

IT'S AMAZING!

The argentinosaurus (below) is the largest land animal ever to be found. It's called the argentinosaurus because fossils of its bones were found in Argentina.

Argentinosaurus (length: up to 35 m)

FLYING REPTILES

While the dinosaurs lived on land, flying reptiles ruled the sky.

These flying reptiles are known as the pterosaurs. They are not dinosaurs, but they lived at the same time as the dinosaurs did.

Eudimorphodon (wingspan: 1 m)

One of the earliest pterosaurs was the eudimorphodon. Inside its beak were small, sharp teeth that helped it to catch fish.

The tapejara was a strange-looking pterosaur. It had a crest on its head that was a metre tall!

Tapejara
(wingspan: up to 5 m)

An enormous pterosaur

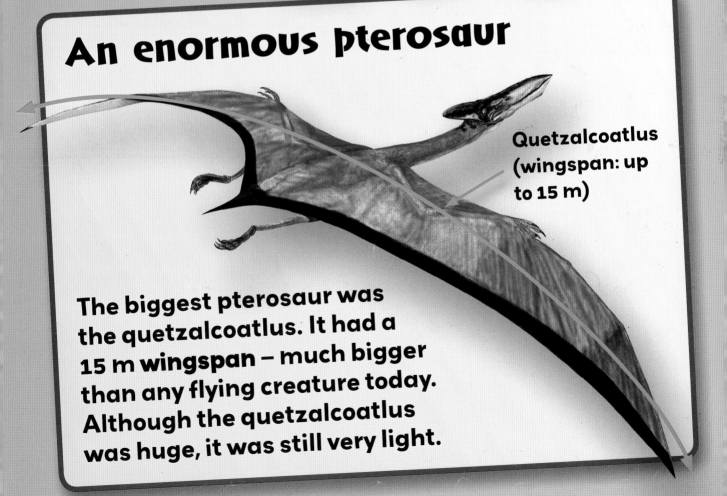

Quetzalcoatlus
(wingspan: up to 15 m)

The biggest pterosaur was the quetzalcoatlus. It had a 15 m **wingspan** – much bigger than any flying creature today. Although the quetzalcoatlus was huge, it was still very light.

DEEP-SEA REPTILES

There was another group of creatures living at the same time as the dinosaurs and the flying reptiles. These were the deep-sea or **marine** reptiles that lived in the water.

Shonisaurus (length: up to 15 m)

The ichthyosaurs were one type of marine reptile. They were the same size as whales are today. For example, the shonisaurus was 15 m long.

Wide eyed!

Ichthyosaurs had huge eyes for seeing underwater. The temnodontosaurus had eyes that were 20 cm across!

The plesiosaurs also lived in the water. There were short-necked and long-necked plesiosaurs. Both had paddle-like limbs for moving through water. The long-necked plesiosaurs really did have long necks – the elasmosaurus's neck was 7 m long!

Plesiosaurus (length: up to 23 m)

EXTINCTION

The dinosaurs became **extinct** (died out) around 65 million years ago. No one knows exactly why, but scientists have several ideas about what might have happened.

Around that time, there were lots of changes happening to the Earth. Many **volcanoes erupted**, and the hot **lava** would have killed dinosaurs and destroyed their **habitats**.

Scientists also think that a huge **asteroid** hit the Earth at this time. The asteroid would have sprayed **molten** rock and ash over the Earth. It would also have changed the climate all over the Earth. This would have caused the dinosaurs and many other creatures to die out.

Crazy ideas!

Some people believe that dinosaurs didn't die out, but were taken by aliens. Others believe they never existed and the bones were planted by aliens as a joke!

ANCIENT CREATURES TODAY

While the dinosaurs became extinct, other creatures that were alive at the same time survived.

Some scientists think that modern birds are related to the dinosaur group called the dromaeosaurs.

A dromaeosaur; Bambiraptor (length: up to 1 m)

Like modern birds (such as this parrot) dromaeosaurs had light, **hollow** bones. They also had feathered arms.

Parrot

Modern crocodiles are related to crocodiles that lived at the same time as the dinosaurs. These were about ten times bigger and heavier than those living today!

IT'S AMAZING!

Dragonflies lived at the same time as the dinosaurs. They look the same today as they did millions of years ago, but they are much smaller!

RECREATING DINOSAURS

Scientists use technology to explain what they think dinosaurs looked like. They can show how they think dinosaurs moved, how they fought, and even what their skin was like.

Film makers use information from scientists to **recreate** dinosaurs for films.

In the *Jurassic Park* films, scientists make dinosaurs live again. The dinosaurs are kept on an island in pens. But they escape while humans are visiting the island!

Of course, no one has ever seen a live dinosaur. So, watching them in TV programmes and films is very exciting.

On-screen dinosaurs!

The television series *Walking with Dinosaurs* was an incredible project. It showed what dinosaurs looked like and how they behaved. It is now an amazing stage show.

GLOSSARY

asteroid a small planet that circles the Sun

carnivore an animal that only eats meat

climate the usual weather in a place

cold-blooded having blood whose temperature changes with the temperature of the air or water. Animals such as fish, snakes and lizards are cold-blooded

continent a large area of land. There are seven separate continents on Earth

desert an area of land that is very hot and dry

erupt to burst out suddenly

extinct no longer living

fossils the remains of animals or plants that have been buried in mud or soil for millions of years

habitat the place where an animal lives

herbivore an animal that only eats plants and vegetation

hollow empty inside

lava hot molten rock that is pushed to the surface when a volcano erupts (blows up)

mammal a warm-blooded animal that makes milk to feed its young

marine to do with the sea

molten turned into liquid by very high heat

palaeontologist a scientist who studies fossils for information about life in the past

plate a hard, flat piece of bone covered with skin that protects the dinosaur

predator an animal that hunts other animals for food

prey an animal that is hunted by another animal

recreate to make again

reptile a cold-blooded animal that has a skeleton and scales or plates on its skin

serrated with grooves or notches in

volcano a landform, such as a mountain or hill, with a hole in the centre through which hot lava and ash are forced out during an eruption

warm-blooded having a body temperature that remains steady and warm, no matter what the outside temperature is

wingspan the distance from the tip of one wing to the tip of the other

FURTHER INFORMATION

Books

Dinosaurs (Usborne Beginners), Stephanie Turnball, Usborne Publishing Limited, 2006.

Dinosaur Discovery: Everything You Need To Know To Become A Palaeontologist, Chris McGowan, Simon & Schuster Children's Publishing, 2011.

Dinosaur Encyclopedia (First Reference), Caroline Bingham, Dorling Kindersley, 2009.

Discover the Dinosaurs, Franklin Watts, 2009.

Websites

Natural History Museum's Dino Directory.
  www.nhm.ac.uk/jdsml/nature-online/dino-directory/
The BBC website all about prehistoric life.
  www.bbc.co.uk/sn/prehistoric_life/
Dinosaur information and puzzles from Dinosaur Jungle.
  www.dinosaurjungle.com/index.php

DVDs

Jurassic Park, Universal Pictures, 1993.

Jurassic Park: The Lost World, 2 Entertain Video, 1997.

Jurassic Park III, Universal Pictures UK, 2001.

Walking with Dinosaurs, Complete BBC Series, 2 Entertain Video, 1999.

INDEX

Note to parents and teachers: Every effort has been made by the Publishers to ensure that the websites on page 31 are suitable for children, that they are of the highest educational value, and that they contain no inappropriate or offensive material. However, because of the nature of the Internet, it is impossible to guarantee that the contents of these sites will not be altered. We strongly advise that Internet access is supervised by a responsible adult.